BLUFF YOUR WAY IN
GOLF

Alan Fulmer
Peter Gammond

CENTENNIAL PRESS

ISBN 0-8220-2225-7
U.S. edition © Copyright 1990 by Centennial Press
British edition © Copyright 1985 by The Bluffer's Guides

Printed in U.S.A.
All Rights Reserved

Centennial Press, Box 82087, Lincoln, Nebraska 68501
an imprint of Cliffs Notes, Inc.

INTRODUCTION

*Golf is a game where the ball always lies poorly
and the player well.*

An Anonymous Bluffer

Golf, it should be stated right away, is no laughing matter.

If you listen to its siren song and get involved, professionally or otherwise, it's very serious business. It can wreak havoc in your life, make a shambles of your home, shatter your self-image, and destroy both your physical and mental health.

If golf is your *modus bluffi,* however, you'll never go to a party worrying about not having anyone to talk to. There's always someone who

(1) plays golf and needs a shoulder to cry on,
(2) plays golf and may be about to give it up,
(3) used to play golf but gave it up because of an incurable slice or a third divorce, or, best of all,
(4) is just about to take it up. This is the ideal victim. You may even be able to sell him your old golf clubs.

Those who are still sane may ridicule this attitude. But never those who are drawn into the web of golf's fatal fascinations.

In addition to committing matrimonial mayhem, the golfer's a frustrated creature who spends life wrestling

3

with the challenge of imposing the virtually impossible upon the improbable. The battle's hardly ever won.

The only thing that can be said in golf's favor is that it gives practiced bluffers plenty of room to maneuver. Before teeing off, even an average bluffer can create a convincing, if fictitious, air of assurance and knowledge that can completely destroy an opponent's confidence. "Shot ten over par last time I was out here. Had a terrible second nine, though!" While actually playing, bluffers can bluff everyone (particularly themselves) with a series of devices which we'll discuss more fully later.

Upon reaching the clubhouse, universally referred to as the 19th hole, as the bitter memories fade and the alcohol begins to have its benevolent effect (all true golfers drink), you can indulge in that form of bluffing that's best categorized as the "distorted memory" and return home glowing in several colors. This doesn't alleviate your loved one's anxiety attacks at all.

"Do you have to leave to play that terrible game again, honey? Leaving me here, alone and sad, to slave over the microwave?"

"Yeah, I promised."

"Don't you care about our marriage? Mother warned me about golfers, but I never thought it would be like this."

"You're being very selfish. I have to stay in shape. Anyway, the club championship is next month and I haven't practiced."

"One day you'll come home to find me gone, the house empty, and the children on the streets."

"Uh-huh, well, I gotta go now. If we don't tee off

by two, it gets crowded. I'll be back in time for supper."

And off she goes to the club, and he returns to the kitchen.

It's a sad little scene that's repeated, with variations, the world over, every day.

GEAR

Bad putting is usually caused by evil spirits.

Michael Green

There are two widely varying philosophies on what "stuff" you really need to play golf. It's universally agreed that you've got to have some clubs and a ball. The question of how many clubs, and what kind, is a much discussed and intellectually stimulating subject. But even before you start handling a club, you have to make two important decisions:

(1) What to carry the clubs around in.
(2) What to wear while you use them.

The go-for-broke (in more ways than one) approach is to impress everyone by having the biggest, best, and most outrageous of all these things. This obviously puts a less well-equipped golfer at a great psychological disadvantage, apart from being distracted by it all.

The other extreme is to carry a light bag with a minimum of clubs. Some of the very best golfers do this and find it an effective tactic. They tend to be the young and athletic ones and always carry the bag over their shoulder. Always be wary of people with a small, ancient bag and a minimum of clubs, especially hickory-shafted clubs. They could be bluffing, of course, but it's just possible that they've discovered the secret of great golf.

Many golfers take a middle-of-the-road approach and simply carry what they really need. These people generally turn out to be average golfers who play average rounds on average courses, and who are continually outsmarted by the not-so-average golfers.

Those who will be "helping" you take your first faltering steps into golf, notably the club professional and his accomplices, will unquestionably favor the impressive approach. So will the manager of the local golf shop, if you choose to purchase your equipment from this source. Although the club professional's probably the greater salesman of the two and will undoubtedly get you to buy more, it's probably best to get most of your things from him in the first place. This will entitle you to be greeted by him on your future visits to the club, and better still, for you to be on "Good morning, Jerry" terms. This obviously makes an impression on any guests you may have with you. Later, you may secretly buy your balls from mail-order houses at half the price, as long as you occasionally buy one or two from Jerry, cheerily explaining that you don't appear to be losing so many lately.

Bags

The first thing you're expected to get is a golf bag, and everyone will try to persuade you to buy the biggest available. It will probably be an enormous leather beast which, in addition to space for clubs, has numerous pockets all over it making it roughly the same shape and size as Dom DeLuise. Try not to get carried away. Unless you play at the kind of exclusive course that employs caddies, you're going to be dragging the thing around yourself. These monster bags are intended mainly for stowing your wardrobe. The pockets decrease in size until the smallest one's a tiny thing with a cute little zipper in which to carry a pencil or a thermometer. There's never any instruction manual for your golf bag. In years to come, you may find that you've been carrying around, in some remote recess, half a bottle of whiskey, a family of mice, and several decaying gloves.

Accessories

What should you put in your expansive and expensive container? First you stuff in all the clothes someone conned you into buying. Clothes which you won't ever actually wear but you think you just might need if, for example, you find yourself stranded on the 5th green in a typhoon. These are so-called waterproof clothes. You're supposed to have three kinds: a light set for summer showers, a medium set for average rainfall, a heavy-duty set for winter blizzards. None of these ever actually keeps the elements out. The secret has either never been discovered or remains intentionally esoteric so that you'll optimistically keep on buying new sets of clothes, thinking you're the only one who hasn't yet discovered the "right" brand. Consequently, you should always carry a towel, preferably two: a big one to dry yourself and a smaller one to dry your clubs.

Hats

Not one, but a variety of hats is essential. A brightly

colored, long-visored one that's one-size-fits-all by means of an inefficient "adjustable" sort of contraption at the back. This hat will make you look like Gary Player or Lee Trevino. You can touch it with the same mock deference they do whenever you manage to sink a problematic putt.

Your second hat should be a wide-brimmed straw hat that ostensibly keeps the sun out of your eyes. This hat should be trimmed with a band of psychedelic colors. A lackluster band is much less effective. As a finishing touch, adorn the thing with a collection of distracting items like feathers, fishing lures, pins with sarcastic slogans, and anything that will make noise when the wind blows.

You might as well also carry a fur hat just in case you're invited on the spur of the moment to play in a tournament in January in Anchorage. You can also add a variety of caps with various densities of plaid according to the prevailing taste or lack thereof.

Umbrellas

Your bag will have a sleeve in which to carry an umbrella. Golfing umbrellas, as even nongolfers know, are huge and generally made up of panels of contrasting primary colors. The only reason for this is distraction. A dull umbrella is a much less effective weapon, even if you snap it up at a critical moment in your opponent's backswing or release it to pinwheel down the fairway in a high wind. It's perfectly possible to get umbrellas, if you know the right people, with advertising slogans on them like "Reach out and touch someone" or "Who could ask for anything more—Toyota!"

You can't do anything more effective, when you're standing near an opponent who's up to his knees in sand, than flourish aggravating slogans. There's no time when he's less likely to want a cuddle, and he's more likely just then to want a bulldozer than a Toyota. So these flashy umbrellas are just the trick to make him twitch on the downswing. Remember though, no golfer would be seen dead with such an object, or a plaid hat for that matter, away from the course. On the course, however, normal human behavior is not expected.

Other Gear

For extreme weather conditions, you should tote a good suntan lotion (about SPF 80) and eye protection equipment ranging from sunglasses to snow goggles. If you've got imagination and a finely developed sense of self-preservation, you'll think of lots of other essentials. For instance, you'll need a thermometer, a barometer, wind and rain gauges, and a compass. You must also keep in mind the possibility that you might get lost in the rough, when it would be sensible to be prepared with a bottle of something sustaining, some basic rations, and a snake-bite kit. Army survival packs are ideal for this sort of emergency. A lightweight tent and some kind of signaling device, like a flare gun or a small foghorn, are also appropriate. You can test the latter periodically to make sure it's in good working order. A good time would be when your opponent is just about to attempt an eight-foot birdie putt.

The thorough golfer also carries a small library, including a guide to the best golf courses (with detailed maps of the course you're playing), a good bar and nightclub guide, the *Official Rules of Golf,*, a current pocket version of the *U.S. Army Psychological Warfare Manual,* spare scorecards, a little pad of paper, several pencils (since they're always getting lost), and a pocket dictionary with colloquial phrases and terms of abuse.

If you try to carry your bag and clubs yourself, you'll be too exhausted to play and possibly disfigured for life. You'll therefore either have to have a caddie (found at the more exclusive clubs or tournaments) or something to put your things on to get around the course. Most people use a pull cart. Nowadays, most clubs insist on one with wide wheels which make it much heavier to pull. Most pull carts remain permanently attached to the bag and "fold up" (with the help of a crowbar and Vise Grips) so that they can be put into the car trunk. A small hydraulic lift might be of some help at this point.

You may therefore be tempted to use an electric or gas golf cart. Although electric carts are wonderful for attaining high speeds on steep slopes, the gas-powered carts are preferable. These roaring behemoths are much more distracting than the most loquacious umbrella or gaudy outfit. Etiquette dictates that all carts should be kept on cart paths and off the tees and greens. But there are no *rules* to keep you from parking close to your opponent's ball. If he asks you to move farther away, you can still make him grind his teeth. Most motorized carts emit a loud screech (similar to fingernails on a chalkboard) when you put them in reverse.

While you're at it, you might as well add one or two other things. A telescopic contraption for retrieving balls out of the water is a good thing to carry with you.

One golfer we know made his pay for itself long ago by charging fifty cents to his one-time friends for each ball he retrieves. At the same time he manages to pick up for himself several more balls drowned by other players. Recently, at a local course, a small pond was drained for cleaning, and over three thousand golf balls were taken from its muddy depths. The golf ball business is always in a bull market.

And in case one of those awful days comes when you arrive at the course to find a notice saying *No Carts,* you should always be sure to have that light bag to carry the two or three clubs you actually need to play.

Clothes

Now that we've dispensed with the spare gear, here are the essentials. Golf is about the only game in the world where people, particularly in the summer, put on more clothes to play than they would normally wear. The guy who cuts his yard in a pair of shorts because of the heat will dress up in order to play golf. The rules at private courses sometimes require it. Lately, there's been a tendency for younger players (and those who have nice knees) to wear shorts — common practice in California and the southern states, but at the more exclusive clubs, it's done with a sense of guilt. Surly pro shop workers will tell you that jeans are not permitted and only shorts of a decent length are allowed.

If you're reasonably dressed in slacks and shirts that were in style in the 70s, the rules of golf don't make any further demands. But custom has it that these clothes be plaids in neon colors. Men and women who are quite conservative at home and in public commonly appear on the golf course in combinations of plaids, stripes, and polka dots, with funny hats, sun visors, and black and white shoes, looking like a 1925 dance band crooner.

Any old sweater is okay for golf, but the majority wear special golf sweaters which have a well-known trademark or the name of a notorious golfer emblazoned upon them. These "exclusive" sweaters usually cost three times as much as similar sweaters without the label.

The golfing glove is also a thing of many colors, all unpleasant. You buy only one of these instead of a pair, which at least saves you money. Gloves are supposed to help your grip. Most players take them off and stick them in their back pockets when they putt, and most would play just as well without a glove, particularly when it gets wet.

As for shoes, you need a lightweight pair for sunny, dry days. For wetter weather, you need a pair of (hopefully) waterproof ones. Only golf shoes which cost $200 or more are even remotely damp resistant. Nowadays some golf shoes look like sneakers, but they have spikes. Spikes may be metal or rubber, supposedly designed to compensate for turf conditions, but really introduced so you'll feel you have to buy four pair of shoes instead of two. As do most other apparel manufacturers, golf shoe magnates feel that looks are much more important than quality craftsmanship, which explains why most trendy golf shoes decay in the first three months you own them.

So you're equipped with fine threads, and you have

a bag full to the brim with life-saving equipment. Now you come to the mechanics of the business and brace yourself to buy a set of clubs.

Clubs

No club professional or golf shop owner would agree, but the only pieces of equipment you need to play a good round of golf are a putter, a sand wedge, a 5-iron, and a ball. Most amateurs would play a better round with just a 5-iron than they do with all the clubs in the world.

The rules of golf state that not more than fourteen clubs may be carried. The golf bluffer usually carries exactly fourteen. This puts him one up on people who carry only thirteen, or six up on those who carry only eight, and so forth. On the other hand, he could be considered to be ten down on the person who carries only four and plays better golf.

Some wise golfers have discovered for themselves that there's hardly any effective difference between a reasonably cheap set of clubs and a very expensive one. They won't be seduced by talk of carbon shafts and steel heads. The average golfer's convinced, however, that only the very best (that is, very expensive) is really good enough for him.

You really don't need a full set of clubs. No amateur golfer uses even half of the clubs that he lugs around to impress his golfing friends. If you walked around carrying just four clubs tied together with a rubber band, you'd probably gain quite a reputation. Unfortunately, most golf clubs insist that each person go out with a full bag. Their main concern is to make the golf shop a profit center so the pro will stay with them.

If you don't want to buy a full set of clubs, you might find some broken ones around the course. You could use just the tops of these to fill up the empty spaces in your golf bag.

Irons

Let's suppose that you've gotten a complete set of clubs. These include a group with metal heads, called irons, numbered 1 through 9. The lower the number the straighter the face. Since only God can hit a 1-iron, and no golfer over a 10 handicap can hit a 2- or 3-iron without driving the ball into the ground or paralyzing his hands, you should regard the 4-iron as the best long iron. Rub dirt and grass on the 1- to 3-irons so they look as if you've used them. An average golfer will have one club somewhere between the 4- and 6-iron which he uses for almost everything. The 5-iron is the favorite. With this, by accident or intent, you may hit a high looping shot, a straight low one, or even putt onto the green in good weather.

Use the 7-iron when you're near the green but not close enough to hit a 9-iron. Nobody uses an 8-iron except by mistake. Obviously the higher numbers are used for shorter shots. If a golfer has a consistent swing, he'll achieve various calculable, diminishing distances from the 1-iron down to the 9-iron.

Golf Story

The golfer says to his caddie, "What do you think? A 7 or a 6?"

The caddie says, "Well, I advised Mr. Peters to use an 8 from here yesterday." So the golfer uses his 8-iron but gets nowhere near the green.

The golfer says, "I thought you said you told Mr. Peters to use an 8-iron from here yesterday?"

"Yes, I did," replies the caddie. "He didn't reach the green either!"

Since average golfers don't have consistent swings, they're likely to sky a 5-iron and top a 9 and thus get the same distance with both. When you top a ball, it's because you've lifted your head to look at a golfer of the opposite sex and hit the ball on the upper edge. This sends the ball six inches into the ground or bounces it along at daisy level. You sky it when you're trying too hard to hit the ball in the air and you hit right underneath it instead. Many golfers have an even more sloping club called a sand iron, or sand wedge, which is really meant (as the name implies) for use in sand traps (the purists always call them "bunkers," so you can too if you want to sound like you know the ropes). Often the pros use it for short shots off the fairway. When amateur golfers do this, the ball usually goes straight up in the air and lands at their feet.

Woods

Now that we've finished the irons, we work our way into the woods (which is very likely where you'll end up). The woods have longer shafts and wooden heads. They're used to hit the ball off the tee and for long shots off the fairway. Professionals use the 1-wood, or "driver," but amateurs should tee off with a 2- or 3-wood to get anywhere at all. Being longer shafted and generally more flexible, the woods tend to give the player more length than an iron. On the other hand, they're much less accurate, and there's an even greater likelihood of missing the ball altogether. Lots of pros use irons off the tee, and it's considered a shrewd thing to do.

But an amateur who uses an iron off the tee is considered to be chicken, incompetent, or geriatric. This means you've got to have a slick spiel ready if you're playing so badly that you don't dare hit your woods.

"Almost always use an iron from here. Bad cross wind. Did you see Tway hit that beauty on television yesterday? 16th wasn't it? Do you mind moving back a step or two? Your shadow's right in front of me . . ."

All of this is in preparation for a weak swing with a 5-iron that doesn't do much except add a stroke to your score.

In the old days, irons and woods had descriptive Anglo-Saxon names like "mashie," "cleek," and "spoon" (see *Glossary*). It's a great asset to be able to use these terms with conviction. Everyone in this mathematical era will be mystified.

Don't forget: no set of golf clubs is complete without a set of covers to go on the woods. You can buy fairly practical but boring ones in the golf shop. Most golfers collect a menagerie of animals and cartoon characters to slip onto their clubs. A fairly practiced bluffer can get several of these puppet heads jiggling and nodding at the same time.

Balls

The original golf ball was a spherical bag made of leather which was stuffed with boiled feathers and made as round as this primitive technology would allow. As golf was played in Scottish cow pastures, certainly this ball felt at home. Frequently these bags split wide open and blew feathers into the players' eyes, no matter which direction they happened to face.

The next ball was made of a rubbery substance called *gutta-percha*, which when heated, could be rolled into a ball and then hardened. These popular balls were known as *gutties*.

As golf became more popular in America, naturally it was an American who invented the modern golf ball. The American ball had a soft core wrapped in several long strings of elastic. The whole ball was then covered with an outer casing of gutta-percha. Conservatives strongly opposed this innovation, but they eventually gave in when the superiority of the new ball allowed their opponents to win with expensive inevitability.

Up to 1921, golf balls were made in various sizes and weights. That year both the Royal and Ancient Golf Club of St. Andrews, Scotland (be sure to offhandedly refer to it as the R&A), and the USGA (United States Golf Association) decided on a regulation ball whose weight was not greater than 1.62 ounces and whose diameter was not less than 1.62 inches. However, in their great tradition, Americans soon got tired of the regulation and decided that their balls ought to be bigger than everyone else's. So the official size was increased to 1.68 inches. Since Americans were better at the game than anyone else, the rest of the world eventually agreed to adopt the new size. But the controversy over whether it was best to have big or little balls raged on for a long time.

The only "advance" in golf ball materials since then is the cheap Japanese ball made of a single solid material, which often breaks into pieces when hit. Each fragment flies off in a different direction with a wicked buzzing noise. The biggest piece is the one that must be played or replaced with another ball, depending on how strictly your opponent interprets the rules. It's rumored that the Japanese are developing balls with tiny computers inside which will be able to make directional changes as they home in on the green. They're not likely to catch on though, since they'll probably cost over $2000 each. Even the most rabid golfer would pause before sending that much money toward a water hazard.

ACTUALLY PLAYING

If you watch a game, it's fun. If you play it, it's recreation.
If you work at it, it's golf.

Bob Hope

The theory, as any golfer will tell you, is very simple. Starting with the clubhead near the ball, you slowly bring it up and behind your head. If you swing it back down on exactly the same path, you're called a professional golfer. All you've got to do to achieve this success is to make sure your feet are correctly placed in relation to the ball, that you're gripping the club properly, that your arms and elbows move through certain prescribed trajectories, that your whole body moves smoothly so that there's no jerking of the club, and that the club comes to the ball in an even, accelerating arc and, after striking, continues over the left shoulder in what's called the follow-through. Oh yes, and you should be perfectly balanced through this entire motion, and your eye should be kept firmly on the ball, head down and unmoving. You keep your head down so golf instructors can laugh at you without your seeing them.

The average person is not naturally adept at keeping his head still while all the rest of him is violently contorting. Most are able to do only one thing adequately at a time. Remembering to do seven or eight things all together in the space of half a second is difficult, even impossible. It also doesn't help to have several people watching you attempt this feat—all of them (with the possible exception of your playing partner) hoping that you'll screw up. Bad golfers are truly happy only when they've gotten away from everyone else and are able to take what they consider to be their natural, easy swing at the ball.

So why not follow the natural, easy swing method? After all, lots of people can hit a nail on the head with a hammer. The trouble is that while you're being natural, you tend to forget the inherent disadvantages of being bowlegged, potbellied, nearsighted, and generally unbalanced. While instinctively compensating for these disabilities, you forget to keep your elbows in, to grip the handle firmly, etc., etc., and the club does not come down the same way as it went up.

At this point, or very soon after, the average golfer becomes completely irrational and decides to try to kill the ball. He slashes wildly with great force. As the ball sails over the adjacent railroad tracks or plops in a pond, the golfer should remember a basic rule in all ball games: If you try to hit a ball hard, it goes nowhere in particular. If it's struck smoothly, sweetly, and with surprisingly little effort, it will go a long, long way.

The second basic rule of golf is "never despair." There's always somebody who's worse than you are. Sometimes you might find this hard to believe, but it's a fact. If you can find such a person, then play with the duffer—as your opponent, of course, not as your partner. The truth is that golf is far more a matter of applied psychology than a matter of physical ability. If you can actually manage to win a hole, it goes without saying that your morale will be high. You will, however, almost inevitably play the next hole badly. But never be foolish enough to play with someone who's a lot better than you are, even on a friendly basis. Some say you should. In tennis, or any game where it's a matter of being in direct opposition, playing somebody better can often enhance your game, even in defeat. But in golf, where it's all up to you, it's courting disaster. The more you try to match their long hits, the shorter and more desperately wayward yours become. If you're the worst player in a foursome, you can become suicidally depressed in no time at all as you constantly trudge along behind, desperately hacking the ball from one trap to the next. Meanwhile, the other three tell jokes (with punchlines excruciatingly similar to your current situation) and compliment each other on the fantastic shots they just made.

The amateur game is roughly based on the professional one—but only roughly. The professional game, when all is going well, is simply a matter of mathematical calculation. A professional (and a low-handicap amateur) always assumes that he's going to hit the ball perfectly, and therefore golf is, to him, only a matter of using the right club. "The distance," says the caddie, "is 135 yards. I recommend a 7-iron, and since the green is slightly tilted to the rear, you'll need some backspin. Oh, and a little fade to the right to allow for the wind." The bluffing golfer will, of course, try to give a similar impression. Right, a 7," he says aloud to himself, "but since the air's a little heavy, I think I'll use a 5. I'll swing easy, open my stance, and fade it to the right." He tops and pulls his ensuing shot, which sends the ball off to the left, and it struggles through a trap, hits a tree stump, and lands near the green. "I was afraid of going over the green, so I used the trap to slow it up," one golfer was heard to say.

That's the kind of thinking that goes on in the average golfer's head. Very rarely does he achieve that frame of mind where he thinks he's going to put it right by the flag. If he did think positively, he'd probably do better. More likely, his troubled mind is saying, "It's a downhill lie, I'm sure to top it, and it'll end up in that trap. So I'm going to play safe and try a gentle lob into the middle of the green, keeping clear of both sand traps in case I hit a line drive." He tops it, and it runs over the green, hits a rake that someone left at the back, and rebounds to within six feet of the pin. The player hastily puts the 9-iron back in his bag and says, as the others come up, "I thought keeping it low was a good idea in these conditions."

The only way to play golf well is to go out with a clear conscience and a clear head. Never speculate about the game. Concentrate on each shot, but don't start thinking you're going to master the course. An old golf adage is "Play the course; don't let it play you." If you can manage a completely nonchalant mood, you might end up playing well. But it's a tough mind-set to pull off.

The Hole-in-One

The most spectacular moment in golf is the hole-in-one. The ball usually goes in the hole in a startlingly erratic and unexpected way. It takes some incredible bounce, ricochets off an unwary woodpecker, or goes screaming over the green only to hit the flag and drop straight in. The observers (and there must be observers or it doesn't count) will either say "Congratulations!" (immediately thinking of the intrinsic drawback – see below) or "What a fluke!" But they're the mean kind, the mean average golfer.

The intrinsic drawback for the hole-in-one golfer, though many are so delighted that they think it's worth it, is that an old custom has it that you have to buy drinks for everyone in the clubhouse. This can be expensive. Consequently, many holes-in-one go unrecorded except on the heavenly scorecard. It follows that the best time to have a hole-in-one is sometime early in the morning, playing with two reliable, tee-totaling witnesses. Get back to the clubhouse before the lunchtime crowd descends.

Putting

Apart from the few arrogant, low-handicap individuals who are good at all parts of the game, golfers are mainly divided into two groups:

(1) Those who are reasonably good at getting to the green but who can't putt to save their lives.
(2) Those who have difficulty in getting to the green but feel happy once they've reached the smooth-cropped surfaces.

Those in the second group can't imagine why so many golfers get bent out of shape (literally) over the simple matter of putting. But if you get onto a green in, let's say, four, then you have a burning desire to get the ball down in only one putt. This induces a state of nervous anxiety and a medley of shakes, quakes, and quivers. To get all that way in four and then take another three shots over the common, family-entertaining pastime of putting is apt to ruin your score and your fun. The happy putter, on the other hand, takes six to get to the same green, is over all his nervous tensions in the rough and the bunkers, and now feels positively lighthearted. He'll often have no difficulty getting the ball in the hole with one smooth putt and, to the annoyance of the twitcher, will halve the hole with him.

So it's often the better golfer who agonizes about his putting, adopts all sorts of strange crouches, and ends up looking like Quasimodo. Some grip their putter a foot from the base, some hold it vertical, some hold it between their legs, some buy six-foot-long putters and stand upright. The worst thing to see is the incurable twitch, a malady known as the yips. This poor guy draws the putter back smoothly, but as it goes toward the ball, the head stops in the middle of the stroke or twists to one side. Overcome by the thought that he's going to miss the hole, he does. But the happy guy has the feeling that he's going to get it down, and he does. Before all golfers looms the specter of the hapless pro who, before a million eyes, missed a short putt and lost a major championship. It would be unnecessarily cruel even to mention the name of Greg Norman, so we won't.

Par or Scratch Score

The par for any given golf course, being far beyond the reach of any average golfer, is always a bone of contention. Verbal viciousness is usually heaped on specific holes—often referred to as a *!%#* long par-4 – a green which a player's supposed to reach in two strokes but will manage that only on miraculous occasions with a strong following wind and drought conditions.

The average golfer will get onto a par-4 in three (two good hits and a chip) and, in order to achieve his par, will have to get down in one putt. It's very hard work and extremely frustrating. When he gets a birdie (one less than the par for the hole), he's exuberant and he'll talk about it for days afterward. His glee is matched only by his description of the one that got away because of the bizarre bounce, sudden gale-force wind, marauding Chihuahua, etc.

Such golfers describe all bogeys (any score over par) as "should've been a par," all pars as "should've been a birdie," and even birdies (may they be forgiven) as "should've been an eagle" (two under par), despite the fact that they have about as much chance of getting an eagle as they do of winning the Publishers Clearing House Sweepstakes.

Rules

No game has more rules than golf. It's an essential part of the bluffer's arsenal not so much to know them all as to know which of them it's necessary to know, along with a handful of irrelevant ones to spout on appropriate occasions. In the days when golf rules were few and simple, there was nothing to be gained by knowing them all because everyone did. The ruling body of golf therefore set up a special team of experts to expand the rules of golf as rapidly (and as confusingly) as they possibly could. The team works diligently at this year in and year out, making sure that the rule book gets bigger and more incomprehensible all the time – particularly the sections on handicapping and scoring.

You might as well carry an old, out-of-date book of rules. No one will ever question its publication date. The fact that it's a book of rules is enough, and if you find a bedraggled, grass-stained copy at a garage sale, people will believe you've pored over it for years. For that matter, you could write your own, and few would know the difference. All golfers stand in awe of the rules (particularly if they've got money bet on the game), but they always do their best to bend them. Some (though we hesitate to admit this) actually cheat!

There's a subtle line between rules and etiquette. There are regulations upon official regulations about what the player can do on the tee, but it's the etiquette part at the end of the book that says, "No one should move, talk, or stand close to or directly behind the ball or the hole when the player is addressing the ball or making a stroke." You can, however, cough, sneeze, or puff on a cigar, shrouding the player in noxious smoke. You could piercingly sing a chorus of "The Impossible Dream" (which is not specifically forbidden). Many of those waiting to tee off regularly sigh deeply and are not penalized.

Here are a few interesting rules you can quote knowingly when the spirit moves you:

- **If the ball oscillates without leaving its original position, it has not moved.** "Hey, your ball moved!" "No it didn't, it only oscillated!" "What do you mean, oscillated?"
- **During the play of a round the player is re-**

sponsible for the actions of his caddie. "Your caddie keeps moving. Do you mind keeping him still? "He didn't move. He only oscillated!" "What do you mean, oscillated?"

- **A caddie is deemed a "loose impediment."**
- **If a ball in motion is accidentally deflected or stopped by any outside agency, it is a rub of the green, no penalty is incurred, and the ball shall be played as it lies . . .** "Hey, you hit my caddie!" "Doesn't matter, he's a loose impediment." "He was only oscillating."

The rule writers wax rhapsodic about some things—hazards, for example. Hazards, after all, are what make golf exciting—flying balls that appear out of nowhere, flying clubs that appear out of nowhere, flying golf bags that . . . But it's the fight against nature that makes the rule makers truly lyrical. For instance, "Interference by casual water, ground under repair, or a hole, cast, or runway made by a burrowing animal, a reptile, or a bird" is what worries them a lot. If a ball encountering one of these is not visible, "the player may probe for it." On the other hand, if he's about to step into a swamp up to his waist, he must not "test the condition of the hazard or of any similar hazard." You'd think they would at least let him put his elbow in it to see if it's too cold. Or jab it with his club to see if there are any water moccasins. In any case, in order to "treat the ball as lost in the hazard, there must be reasonable evidence that the ball is lodged in it." If it's been swallowed by an alligator living in the hazard, there's not much you can do about it, and the rule makers aren't very helpful. They'll pursue a point just so far, but then you're on your own.

28

Cheating

Cheating's been known to happen in golf. Not, we should add, by us personally or anyone that we know and play with – honest. And what little cheating there is, isn't earthshaking – just a little manipulation, sometimes accidental.

Cheating off the tee is tough, at least on the part of the player when he's being watched by beady-eyed opponents. So, more often than not, it's the opponent who'll cheat (if you care to call it that) by a well-timed hiccup or by inexplicably tripping over his golf bag and loosing a cacophony of clubs. Some blatantly talk, but you can usually stop them with a contemptuous look. A common bluffing opportunity arises if you miss the ball altogether – what's technically termed a *whiff* and counts as a stroke if you're playing strictly by the rules. To avoid the penalty, you should always take a practice swing so everyone gets used to the idea. It's even better if your real swing has the appearance of being a practice swing so that your unconcern seems natural. The trouble with this ploy is that a real swing that looks like a practice swing usually turns out worse than a genuine practice swing, because the practice swing's unpressured.

Down the fairway, the opportunities for a little entrepreneurial maneuvering increase. In fact, the worse your shot and the greater the distance from the other players, the more you can do. In winter or bad conditions, you're allowed to move the ball a short distance if it's in a hole or somewhere you don't like very much. You should therefore always move the ball as a matter of principle until someone says, "Hey, there's no winter rules." You can then innocently apologize.

Checking your ball to be sure it's yours is a common dodge. Turning it to see whether it has "Property of the Longwood Driving Range" written on it, or even a particular brand name, you can move it ever so slightly to a better position. This works especially well in the short rough. The fact that you know perfectly well that it's your ball shouldn't stop you. The rules of golf are so strict that if you don't check your ball and you end up playing someone else's, you're heavily penalized.

If the ball has landed in the thick rough and you get there before anyone else, some slight adjustment of the lie is almost beyond resisting. The honorable bluffer wouldn't do anything unscrupulous (such as moving the ball toward the hole), but others might. You *can* move loose dead branches away. "Oh my, how unfortunate. The ball rolled right out of that ground squirrel hole." Totally depraved players, we suspect, might even have another ball ready to drop through a hole in their pants pocket.

The sand trap is the natural habitat of the sleight-of-hand artist—not only because of those forbidding walls of sand and overhanging grass, but mainly because in a sand trap you must not "ground" the club. In layman's terms, that means that it must not touch the sand before you've swung the club, although it may hit the sand first during the stroke.

On the green, manipulation is minimal. Of course, you're allowed to pick up your ball to clean it, and you can gain a few inches this way. Always put the marker down in front of the ball, but replace the ball in front of the marker. Even professionals do this because nobody pays much attention to the action. Never be seduced by a patronizing "Why don't you putt out so you don't have to mark it?" It's a well-known saying that a putt taken in haste is oft repented. That's what your opponent hopes. On the other hand, marking an eighteen-inch putt will leave your opponent with his four-footer in a state of uncertainty. And you can easily disrupt his concentration with the nominally well-meaning but startling cry "Do you want the flag out or tended?" Better yet, try the apparently friendly "Don't leave it short," "A lot of golf there still," or "Get it close." Putting is entirely in the mind. On a bad day, even the best can be verbally nudged toward catastrophe.

Leagues

Groups of golfers, tired of playing with Joe, Marge, and Ted, form themselves into a league in order to play one day a week for 12 to 36 weeks depending on the group's stamina and masochistic tendencies. Leagues are often formed by people who work at the same company. These gluttons for punishment would rather spend another couple of hours a week with their coworkers than with their spouses or children. Leagues are welcomed by most golf courses because they provide a guaranteed income. But they're not appreciated by the members of the club where they're playing (like Joe, Marge, and Ted) because it upsets their weekly game.

The league is tirelessly organized by a secretary who has run it for ten years and seems to get some sort of perverse pleasure out of it—and a sleeve of golf balls, a word of thanks from the current league president, and a round of applause upon retirement.

Everyone plays worse than they usually do on their own well-beloved courses, and it inevitably rains for at least 50 percent of the matches. Leaving their chicken-scratched, often soggy scorecards with the secretary and his long-suffering assistant, the golfers retire to the bar, where the golf club tries to make as much money as possible. At the end of the year, there's a token dinner, from which the golf club tries to make as much money as possible. Trophies are handed out to the best and worst in every imaginable category. Insincere thanks are rendered to all, and off they go, back to their office cubbyholes, leaving the make-believe golf match world behind. Those who go home to their loved ones indulge in their final bluff of the day when they behave as though the six balls they won as a door prize at a cost of $30 were, in fact, an amazing treasure that made the whole thing worthwhile.

The golf bluffer is in his element in a league. Since many leagues insist on a maximum allowance of strokes, your handicap is lowered. You can therefore bask in being a 20, but it usually ruins your chances of winning. There's great deal of confusion over handicaps anyway, and many bluffs are made and called at the expense of the league secretary. Each night the air is alive with stories of what golf magic various players have performed elsewhere, unlike today when they had a blister on their thumb, accidentally broke their 5-iron by bashing it repeatedly against a tree, or were paired with Attila the Hun. The winners can hardly believe their luck.

GOLF COURSES

*Golf is a game where a man places a small sphere
on top of a larger sphere and attempts to
dislodge the small sphere from the top of the larger sphere.*

Anon.

The best golf courses supposedly subject a player to
an excruciating trial of strength and character – one of
life's great adventures, spoken of in the same rever-
ent tones that men use when they speak of being in
"WW two – the Big One." It's a justified comparison that
sounds like this:

"It was on the Palm course at Disney World that I
got one of my best pars. On the 18th, I think. Par-4,
454 yards. Almost hit my drive into the fairway
trap. Hit an awesome, hooking 6-iron. Bounced off
a tree and landed right on the green. Should've
been a birdie, but it just curled around the hole.

"Yessir, reminds me of Pebble Beach. Playing up
the 18th, I hit a hook, and the ball goes out toward
the rocky coastline. Thought I'd lost it, but it hit
the rocks and bounced right back into the middle
of the fairway. 11th's the worst hole I've played,
though. Blind shot off the tee and sand traps like
trenches. Ended up taking a nine there."

"What about the 10th at Pleasant Valley?"

"Not as bad as the 15th at Oak Hill."

"Does it compare with the 2nd at Pinehurst?"

"What about the 4th at Firestone? I went into the trees there and it took me nine to get out."

"If you get into the trap at the 17th at PGA West, it's all you can do to climb up to the ball, let alone hit it."

And so it goes. For those who still carry the scars of those hard-fought campaigns, each heartfelt stroke is seared into memory. Listening to these conversations, you can almost see John Wayne begrimed with sweat and gunpowder and hear the strains of "America" rising to a crescendo.

You must accept the fact (however difficult it is to believe) that golf courses are actually *planned* by people known as golf course designers. It's depressing to contemplate the depths of cunning, treachery, and ruthlessness that must prompt such people to inflict so much anguish on those who are as sensitive and as easily wounded as golfers. This form of sadism is also rampant among those who choose *Driver's Test Examiner* as a career field.

Imagine two such characters who have been asked to turn a swamp, mountain, or shaggy woodland into a golf course. Listen — if you can bring yourself to — to their tortuous discussion as they pick their untroubled way through the underbrush.

". . . That would be a great 1st. Nothing like a wide dip in the fairway to make distance hard to figure. We'll leave the creek at the bottom. Next one will make a nice dogleg. They won't know about that quarry until they come around the corner . . ."

"Now there's a nice long hike for a par-5. That'll instill a feeling of hopelessness. A short one here, I think. Some of them are bound to go over the back and into that bunch of poison ivy. Nice tilt on the fairway there to throw them into the trees. Then a gentle curving one. They're sure to try to cut the corner, and if we leave that pine there, 60 percent will hit it."

"Look! A pond full of lilies. What about a short one over that, with a green sloping back toward the water and the flag right on the edge? Dredge it every month and the club will make a nice profit in balls. A deep ditch across this fairway. Leave the swamp beyond it. No warnings. Just a 'ground under repair' sign. They're bound to ignore it."

"Now a good uphill climb. Hole will always be known as Heart Attack Hill. To finish, what better than a narrow passage through the trees, and the final green right in front of the clubhouse. Don't forget to insure the windows heavily."

"You still think the 12th was too straightforward? That's okay. Give 'em one to raise their hopes. Anyway, we can keep the rough pretty long. Want to play a game of golf next week?"

"No thanks, gave it up years ago . . ."

Overheard on the Radio

Announcer: Dave, which would you pick as your particular favorite?

Dave: Oh, I think without a doubt the 5th. Formidable to approach in many ways, and it's gotten a lot of criticism. People get lost on that last rough stretch, but it's really satisfying when you manage it just right.

Announcer: Pete?

Pete: I agree, basically, but I still like the 9th. You've got to have rhythm to avoid all the traps. But once you negotiate those, the magnificient serenity of the approach is very appealing.

Announcer: John?

John: I think the 1st sets the pattern for the rest. Not seeing the final objective adds a lot to the challenge here. Right away you're among the trees, so to speak.

Dave: Yeah, but it's heavy going. Almost too much of a challenge too early.

Pete: It's strange that we all pick the odd numbers. The 4th, the 6th, and 8th all have contrasting attractions. Less demanding maybe but plenty of hazards.

John: I'll always remember the first time I faced the 8th. I needed a couple of creative, perfectly timed strokes.

Announcer: So far we've only discussed the early sequence. Don't you think that after the 9th, the more complicated twists and turns add a new dimension?

Dave: Sure. The massive 11th, in particular, poses unique problems. But it's so satisfying to overcome them. Even when you've reached the target, it's difficult to hold. It can fall away at the end if you're not careful.

Pete: And by the time you reach the hair-raising 13th, your momentum may have disappeared. Your attention can wander at that point.

John: Even so, the maze of the 11th always leaves us hungry for more.

Announcer: Well, thank you, gentlemen. I hope we've set the scene for some fascinating perform-ances this week. Pete, as one who's played all of these, what do you predict?

Pete: I think it's going to be a fascinating ex-perience.

Announcer: Well, thank you, Dave, Pete, John, and thank you at home for listening. The broad-casts of the complete cycle of Shostakovich sym-phonies will be aired each night for the next two weeks. We'll be back "Talking Music" next week at the same time.

Clubs

Not the kind you play with, like woods and irons, but the kind you join or go to with names like Wood Haven, Iron Mountain, Ironwood, or other monnikers evocative of healthful air, respite from stress, and fron-tier spirit all at the same time.

Golf courses always fit into one of three descriptive and net-worth-conscious pigeonholes: private country clubs, semiprivate clubs, and public golf courses.

Private Clubs

The private clubs take themselves excruciatingly seriously—more than they do in any other sport. These clubs are becoming both more exorbitantly priced and less and less particular about the blueblood background of applicants for membership. This makes it extremely difficult for the novice bluffer because distinguishing the bluebloods from the crassly *nouveau riche* from the bluffing hoi polloi is an exacting skill.

Don't be intimidated. Even though bluffing your way in this rarified atmosphere is like being pushed onto a Broadway stage without warning to sing a medley from *The King and I,* enter these clubs with upright posture, hawklike gaze, self-confident demeanor, and stentorian voice. But while your voice may be loud, your clothes should not. Stash all that gaudy golf apparel you bought to fit right in with the crowd at the Wahoo, Nebraska, William Jennings Bryan Municipal Golf Course and Water Slide. Most members and the club pro will expect you to dress in conservative slacks with an open-necked shirt and the monogrammed sweater that's the course's trademark.

On your first few visits, study the prevailing pecking order with special care. In some clubs, you'd better speak to even the bartender with a degree of humble respect. "No, ma'am, I'm afraid we don't serve that kind of thing in here," he may say, and you're not sure whether he's referring to your order for a wine cooler or to your brother-in-law. Be quick to assert your superiority or you'll find yourself being humble to greenskeepers, starters, rangers, and even the club professional.

There's a legend (carefully nurtured by those in

financial circles) that belonging to a country club, and thus mingling with potential associates and customers, is a desirable thing. Some banks and businesses, for example, actually encourage their managers to play golf every day. The only ones who object are those who hate golf. But we've got to come clean—while you'll hear comments like "If I didn't play golf, I'd never have unloaded that old house and motel on Norman Bates. Bought the house for his mother. They're close, you know. Talked it over while we were waiting at the 12th . . ." Don't believe a word of it.

No one has ever conducted or acquired any business on a golf course or in a clubhouse, primarily because they're much too busy discussing their swing or their putting stance, or they've made Jim Beam or Johnny Walker their playing partner for the day.

Semiprivate Clubs

The semiprivate courses do a sometimes painful balancing act by trying to meet the needs and surly demands of both their own members and their public customers. Any owner of a semiprivate club is a candidate for ulcers and high blood pressure. But the payoff for these owners is the fact that they can charge the public any price they want—and as soon as they get enough money, they'll go private.

Public Courses

Public courses are the least expensive places to learn or play golf. These courses are typically municipally owned to create jobs for people who don't know anything about maintaining a golf course. Privately owned public courses usually have some other shortcoming. They have only 9 holes instead of the customary 18, or they were built over the retired site of the old sewage treatment plant and radioactive waste depot (where you can play until midnight because your clubs glow in the dark). In either case, no one with an IQ above 60 or even a modest sense of style plays on them, so the owner remains a borderline pauper and the course remains a borderline blight. It's doomed to remain a step below the semiprivate courses and a step (just) above miniature golf.

Public courses very often have their bar windows overlooking the first tee. This sadistic practice makes it obvious that most golf clubs, whatever their priorities, expect their golfers to be able to play the game (and are not above using the most spectacular klutzes as 19th hole entertainment). All that really matters in this situation is that you respectably get off the first tee and out of sight of the other golfers. How you manage that is your own business. Nobody can help. But taking your second shot five yards from the clubhouse and your third from the center of a lilac bush four yards from that, is the most humbling of human experiences. Golfers who've had this experience more than once generally try to bribe someone to let them start on the second tee beyond the sight of the smirking kibitzers.

But despite their shortcomings, public courses are pleased to admit anyone, no matter what their ability and background may be. Here, those whose only real failing is that they can't play golf rub shoulders with artisan golfers. Only undying love of the game makes that bearable for either side.

The Tournament

Most of the golfer's life (and money) is spent in preparation for the great day – the golf tournament. The day when he feels sure that he'll triumph over adversity and at least win a sleeve of three golf balls of a kind he doesn't ever use.

A golf tournament is designed to make as many people as possible unhappy. Not just one or two as in most sports, not even nine or eleven – but perhaps as many as seventy people at a time (which is about the size of golf tournament that the average golf club can't quite cope with). In the end, only one of the hopefuls has any claim to fame. But even these winners, draped in exhaustion across the clubhouse bar, will bemoan the fact that they just failed to better their previous best score or that they *just missed* the hole-in-one by a matter of inches.

The second place finishers are the saddest to see. It's never their fault that they put the ball into the water on the 15th. Their hopes have been shattered, and they've once more missed the golden opportunity of taking home the tallest of the fake walnut veneer and gold-toned plastic trophies that were mistakenly engraved *Hillsdale Country Flub Tournament*. Third place finishers are hardly any happier, having won yet another striped umbrella to add to the six they already have in the garage.

The tournament organizers are unhappy because some viciously inventive criticisms have been leveled at them. The club owners are unhappy. They always are. Even the club cat is unhappy because there's nowhere to sit. The poor soul who comes in seventieth and earns the booby prize is the happiest. At least bring-up-the-rears know there's no greater degradation they can be subjected to and now there's nowhere to go but up.

Everyone vows to give up the game forever. Then they have another drink and lay out the planning sheets for the next tournament.

GOLF PLAYERS

Have you ever noticed what golf spells backwards?

Al Boliska

Strangely enough, little has been written about the golf mentality. Plenty has been said about its techniques, equipment, courses, and star players, but almost nothing about its motivations and associated attitudes. If you know just a little about the Zen of golf, you'll be in a strong position in any golf conversation. The bluffer who actually considers the game of golf in a Freudian context is a devastating opponent for those whose conversational base consists of the size of their balls, their swing, and the advisability of the questionable things they did on the 15th hole last Thursday.

Motivation and Associated Attitudes

What perverse and compelling personality disorders lead people to play golf, and what are the psychological and domestic failures that are the inevitable outcome? Take, for example, the position of the fallible golfer standing on the first tee in a state of pessimistic expectancy, surrounded by hostile interest, with rain (or some other meteorological hazard) assailing his being. In this already unfavorable situation, he must hit a small hard ball with a poorly conceived appliance toward a hole that's so distant it may be invisible to his ageing optics, or possibly not even in sight at all. There's a fifty-fifty chance that the ball will end up in a prairie dog's stomach, a squirrel's nest, or eventually another golfer's pocket, but he really doesn't care about that. All he fervently wishes for is that it goes a long, long way. If it's straight down the middle, fine. It's very manly or golfing-womanly to hit a long shot, even if it's never seen again. It's a sign of debility to hit something weakly or not at all. (*Debility:* an enfeebled state, a particular mental or physical handicap – a condition common to the average golfer.)

It can be assumed that golfers play golf to prove that they can mentally overcome the pressures that golf puts upon them. The fact that if they didn't play golf at all they wouldn't *have to* endure or overcome its pressures doesn't occur to them.

So what gets them out there in the first place? Some say that golfers golf in order to get away from their marital partner. This theory is supported by the fact that 99 percent of all golfers are married. You'll rarely meet an unmarried one. There's also a certain degree of status in playing the game. After all, if you're playing golf at 10 o'clock on a Tuesday morning, you can hardly be considered a wage slave (and you don't have to make it common knowledge that you're "between engagements"). But although golf is indulged in by such diverse types as seamstresses and CEOs, it still has a solidly middle-class feel. The average amateur starts playing golf because he's no longer fit enough to play the active games of his youth, like football and raquetball, or even those "signs of decline," like tennis and jogging. The only place where the average golfer breaks into a fast walk is between the 18th green and the clubhouse. If he ran, he'd never make it.

It's clear that one of the reasons for playing golf is to claim the benefits of the physical activity and fresh air. Playing a sport and breathing air in spite of an increasing waistline, poor eyesight, weak heart, varicose veins, and high blood pressure is a defiant gesture by people who otherwise expend their energies on drinking beer (known as "pumping aluminum").

Golfing Types

Either you're a golfer or you're not. You can't be mildly interested in golf anymore than you can be mildly pregnant. (By the way, it's not true that pregnant women give up the game because they have difficulty seeing the ball; the truth is that no one's come up with a drop-dead golf maternity outfit.) Just as with alcoholics, gamblers, and *Star Trek* fans, the commitment must be total. That's why the game's played by such a strange race of men and women.

The average golfer will never actually meet, let alone play with, the truly adept practitioners – they'll all be playing in tournaments. The strange thing is that all the best players in golf, or tennis, or what-have-you never seem to practice. They just appear, with their low handicaps and their custom clubs, knocking the ball perfectly down the middle of the fairway. Young, fit, and arrogant golfers don't play with average golfers. They could all be professionals, but they don't want to. They don't hang out in bars. They wear perfectly fitting yellow and green outfits that you wouldn't dare be seen in, yet these people are bronzed and agile. To be spoken to by a good player is worth several strokes off your own game.

Golf is a mental game as much as a physical one, at least at the average level — a fact that becomes obvious when you take a look at the proficiency (or lack of it) exhibited by various occupational types. Doctors, lawyers, and other professionals generally seem to be pretty good at golf and hover around a 10 handicap. They treat golf as they treat their clients — with a sort of disdainful superiority. They're not the kind of people who let golf get the upper hand. Banking executives, because they play six or seven times a week, can be good at the game, but they're more fallible. Their off days coincide with days when the dollar has fallen or interest has gone up or they've mislaid something — like the million-dollar trust fund they've been personally administering. Artistic types fluctuate even more. Actors (particularly comedians) often have low handicaps, which are usually a more accurate reflection of their inventive powers and improvisational techniques than their golf acumen. Engineers, contractors, and owners of demolition businesses generally have a bullheaded approach, which stems from their occupations. If you get it right, great. If you get it wrong, get a bigger hammer (or driver). Retailers and farmers tend to have a steady, down-the-middle kind of attitude. They don't hit it far, but they stay in the fairway.

The Short, Fat, and Rounded

Many variations of short, plump, hamsterlike men and women play golf. Lacking the midriff flexibility of the young and lean, they develop highly personal styles. The short backswing is the most usual. This, in the hands of some professionals and amateurs, can be an effective and accurate tool, but it rarely achieves length and can lead to other defects, like too quick a downswing. The small, round golfer is frequently aggressive.

The Long and Lean

These golfers can manage a fuller, larger arcing swing but tend to appear contorted, with arms and legs fighting a civil war for supremacy and direction. They can be great hookers and slicers.

The Purist

This one reads and knows the rules. All of them. Rulemongers are menaces to play with. They know no greater joy than pointing out to you loudly, and in an inevitably piercing, nasal voice, that they hate to be the one to mention it, but they really don't think the rules allow you to count yourself as a burrowing animal—even though you've dug yourself two feet deep in that trap.

The Know-It-All

The sworn enemy of the bluffer, the know-it-all harangues you about his supposed expertise on the technicalities of golf. He especially takes delight in detailing what you should do in sand traps and water hazards. He's no great shakes in these situations himself, but he's always ready to give you the benefit of his instruction. The trick is to ask him if he'd mind stepping back fifty yards or so because you keep seeing him out of the corner of your eye. He'll take this

personally, and with luck, he may never speak to you
again.

The Slow and Steady

Usually this one is middle aged or older. She's learned
by experience that there's no sense in trying to send
the ball to the moon. Having repeated "slow and steady"
to herself metronomically and interminably over the
years, she's at last become *sooooo* slow and *sooooo*
steady that you'll wonder if she's a Disney animatronic
with rusty gears.

The Talker

One of the worst golfers to play with, although he
may be a nice guy and the life of the party, is the
nonstop chatterer. Weaned on the obligatory butt-
slapping, jaw-flapping fraternization of the baseball
field, he's brought his adolescent camaraderie to the
fairways and to you. Ignore him if you can, which
might—just might—shut him up eventually. But always
keep in mind that he may be a master bluffer who has
read our discussion of distractions with particular care.

The Easily Agitated

Be careful what you say and do around this one. Her
first and most accessible reaction to frustration is to
throw her club. Surrounded by a tree-lined fairway, she
can create a tense situation as she chucks a club into
the awaiting branches and then spends the next fifteen
minutes getting other clubs stuck in the trees in an
effort to free the first club. The situation can also become a great deal more serious than this with an invet-
erate equipment flinger. (Remember the incident of the

player with a snapped iron shaft through the jugular?) For your continued health, both mental and physical, avoid this individual. One of the most long-lasting ways to do that is to goad her into intemperance just as she reaches a large pond. Once she deposits her entire bag into the muck, she won't be able to continue and you can go your separate ways.

The Sandbagger

This one is out to win. He frequently plays for money and often flaunts a high handicap that he's slyly accumulated from a number of bad rounds played for fun. This creative flair allows him to win both tournaments and side bets. The sandbagger is sneered at by everyone and is commonly seen as a "pirate." The only reason he doesn't beat everyone with this cunning subterfuge is that most of the people he plays with are "pirates" too.

The Athlete

A young, bronzed type – the kind you love to hate. She takes golfing holidays in Hawaii, plays softball and tennis, water-skis, and runs cross country. She has a husband who looks like Arnold Schwarzenegger and who finds it amusing to hold up their Land Rover with one hand while she changes a tire. Often she'll carry her golf bag with just a few efficient-looking clubs in it. Frequently her first remark is "Haven't played in six weeks." She then proceeds to hit long, accurate shots, putting with surgical precision and shrugging off praises for her birdies with aggravating modesty. Don't play with her. Ever. You don't want to become one more anonymous suicide statistic.

The Good Sport

In case we seem to be loading things rather heavily against the bluffing golfer, there's also the nice golfers (Honest Joe and Jane), who duff away uncomplainingly, naively delighted when they hit a good shot, and even express admiration when other people achieve good things. These amazing people are truly rare. If you find one, hang on.

Clyde

A Clyde is an essential item in anyone's golfing life. Since the best way to bluff your way through a round of golf is to play with someone who's guaranteed to be more erratic than you are, there's a great demand for the company of a Clyde. Your Clyde might be called Estelle, Dave, Susan, or Vern—but for the moment, let's stick with Clyde.

Clydes do have the capacity (usually extremely well hidden) to be good players. Our particular Clyde is a well-built guy who has the strength to hit the ball for miles. He's generally very reliable, helpful, and friendly away from the golf course. Occasionally, he executes a well-directed swing and the ball goes a long, long way. Apparently he hits these shots with his eyes closed. He's even been known to get a birdie, and his simple elation on these occasions is heartwarming to behold. It's always a pleasure when Clyde wins a hole.

Unfortunately, these triumphs always have a kind of Jekyll-and-Hyde effect on him. He seems to forget that he's Clyde and happily answers to the name of Gary, Arnold, or Jack. He delivers the next drive with a wild ferocity and power that moves everyone back a step or two. Shoulders hunched, he really means to

smash that ball. If he actually makes contact, it's likely to go even farther than before but in such a variety of uncontrolled directions that the only sensible place to be is cringing behind the golf cart, well behind him. Even that isn't a guarantee of safety.

The final resting place of these shots is signaled by an explosion of startled crows, a distant splash, the sound of breaking glass, or cries of anger and anguish from a nearby fairway. Clyde, who reads a lot of books about golf, explains in a few brief technical terms to the silent spectators that he wasn't lined up correctly (which everyone could see anyway) or that something slipped.

Even more often, his ball bounces along the ground for a few yards or burns a few worms and then mysteriously buries itself in a pristine area of the fairway that would seem to offer no cover at all and is never seen again.

Recently, Clyde drove his first tee shot into a sand trap. It happened to be a sand trap on the nearby 9th, and a foursome completing their first nine displayed signs of hostility to this muscling in on their turf. After three shots to get out of the trap—so deeply had the ball burrowed—and another two to get a hundred yards down the fairway, his morale was understandably low, and he wasn't responding well to the gleeful gibes of his companions. It took him several holes to recover his good nature.

Clyde's always worrying about how many over five he is at each point on the course. He rarely has to think in terms of being under. Having scored 45 on the first five holes, he's apt to get depressed. Sometimes even violent. You can't help but feel that it'd be better if he didn't dwell on the score so much. Away from the golf course he's such a gentle guy.

Clyde's the only golfer who's ever lost five balls on the first tee. This happened at one of those very expensive country clubs often frequented by retired comedians and CEOs of companies with cost plus contracts with the federal government—having what they describe on their income tax as a business lunch. Now Clyde is never careless in his approach to golf. Where guys like Trevino might just step up to the ball and slap it down the fairway, Clyde prepares for his drive with great thoroughness. He shuffles his feet with the virtuosity of Gregory Hines; then he aligns his rear and indulges in fifteen preliminary waggles of the club. He then takes off his glasses and cleans them and goes through the entire routine again. On this particular day, he went through his compulsive countdown as usual. The half-dozen foursomes waiting to go off behind him were clearly impressed and expected something spectacular after such a thorough preparation, since both comedians and CEOs have usually reached their rarified status with this same attention to detail.

The first four lost balls were simply a matter of that golfer's disease, especially virulent on the first tee, known as topping. Each of them went into the thick and almost impenetrable wilds of foot-long grass that are a picturesque feature of this particular course. A concerted effort by everyone in the vicinity (including a private detective) failed to reveal their location. Given the increasing violence of the blows they'd been dealt, they were probably wisely hiding in the dark a yard beneath the surface of the sandy subsoil.

The ever-growing crowd of backed-up players,

though definitely interested, were beginning to mutter and mumble among themselves. But, generously they agreed that Clyde should have another chance. In fact, they were probably fascinated by what might happen and were intent on boosting their own egos by watching somebody who was more spectacularly incompetent than they could possibly dream of being. They weren't disappointed. Professional golfers can put quite a bit of backspin on the ball with a wedge, but Clyde achieved the same effect with his driver. His club went so low and hard under the ball (presumably known as *bottoming*, although we haven't come across the word) that it acquired a phenomenal amount of backspin. While Clyde stared with a puzzled expression down the fairway, the ball actually went backwards, streaking like a Stinger missile through the waiting golfers. The attack of the killer Dunlop was not applauded, but everyone agreed that they'd never seen anything like it in their lives. It provoked interminable discussion, since it was a situation which nobody remembered seeing in the rule book. It was finally decided by the local pro that, since Clyde's ball was now on the 18th fairway, all those waiting to go off the first tee were entitled to do so (and hopefully get clear) before he played his next shot.

Twenty minutes later, Clyde went back into action. The rest of his foursome were ready to quit and hoist a few Heinekens, but Clyde's enthusiasm was still high. On the edge of overt irritation, he refused to indulge in any half measures like playing safe with an iron. Fortunately, he now hit a powerful, zooming, incredibly long shot (as he sometimes does on unexpected occasions) which homed in on a rarely used sand trap about two hundred yards down the left of the fairway. He became even more militant. Stepping into the trap, he skipped his usual preparations and hacked at the ball with a wedge and with intense, repressed ferocity. It flew out of the sand, very high and surprisingly far, soaring over a line of trees and out of bounds into a swimming pool belonging to a television celebrity. He was in it at the time. The ball didn't actually hit the celeb, but his hostile remarks seemed pretty excessive for someone who has to maintain a good public image.

Clyde was firmly persuaded not to go and ask for his ball back and was allowed a free drop.

Golf is never dull when you're playing with a Clyde. For that matter, golf is rarely dull at any time. Maddening, sickening, frustrating, hateful, yes, but never dull.

HANDICAPS

I play in the low 80s.
If it's any hotter than that, I won't play.

Joe E. Lewis

One of golf's best features, one that holds the most possibilities for the serious student of bluffing, is one that has little to do with playing. It's referred to as the handicapping system.

In theory, handicapping allows an average or poor player to compete on even terms with the very best, even a scratch player. This gritty term describes a player who's considered capable of playing a par-72 course in 72 strokes. All professionals are euphemistically classified as scratch players. An average player might find that her score week after week is about 98, more or less. She'd then be a 26 handicap player. Theoretically, if Nancy Lopez and one of us played our local course together, she'd shoot 72 and we'd shoot 98 and the game would be a draw. In reality she'd probably shoot 69 and we, playing in a state of high anxiety in her august presence, would shoot 117. But that's beside the point.

The amateur player's handicap is based on scorecards that he's submitted after playing with other members of the course. Not those which he's filled out while playing with his drinking friends or by himself or those he's vividly fantasized about.

The situation's complicated by the fact that there are two kinds of golfers, an honest minority and a dishonest majority. The honest minority report a handicap that reflects their true ability and make it a point of honor to see that it's adjusted if they're playing well. You may never meet one of these paragons, but they do exist, mostly in the form of club committee members who have to be careful.

The handicap system causes the most bitterness in leagues, where everyone suspects everyone else and the only person who's generally liked is Clyde or his equivalent. The highest imaginable handicap for a player in most leagues is set between 20 and 26 depending on the caliber of the players. So the duffer whose *real* handicap is about 50 is never going to beat anybody.

Very rarely, when asked before a match what his handicap is, will a player say, simply and concisely, 26 or 10. He'll say, "Well, actually I'm a 26 . . ." which carries the implication that he's more like a 20 (which might be true in good double bluffing tradition). He might say, "I play to a 26," which somehow suggests that he's actually about a 32 but is forced to conform to a 26 handicap that he acquired one lucky day (or unlucky day, depending on your point of view).

On the other hand, both statements might imply the exact opposite, according to whether the golfer looks you in the eye or not. The lower the handicap, the more likely it is that the player will be pleading his own cause. "I've got a 10 handicap" suggests a degree of doubt in the player's mind and a probable ability of about a 16. No golfer at that level is likely to say he's a 10 when he's really a 4. He just couldn't bring himself to do it. What he's more likely to say (truthfully or not) is

"Well, I used to be a 4, but now it's more like a 10."

"Are you saying you're a 10?" his opponent asks.

"That's my present handicap," he'll reply, and the opponent now doesn't know whether to expect golf of a 4- or 10-handicap standard. It'll probably be a 16.

The phrase "Well they've given me a 20 handicap" can be proclaimed by someone who's capable of playing to a 15 on a good day, someone incapable of anything better than a 40, or an egotist who likes to say 20 when he's really a 24.

The muttering gets loudest as the 26 handicapper goes up to collect the trophy or the golf bag at the end of the day's tournament. Ominous rumblings also accompany the success of the cocky 4-handicapper who's actually played to it. It's a loaded subject.

PROFESSIONALS

The only reason I ever played golf in the first place was so I could afford to hunt and fish.

Sam Snead

One of the finest things about golf is that the worst amateurs are allowed to play on the same courses as the most revered professionals. One day you may be scurrying around ruining the fairway, and the next day you may watch Tom Watson in the same spot, taking even greater divots, but intentionally.

If you can afford to go and watch the professional tournaments, you won't be seated in nosebleed territory at the top of the stadium as you might be in other sports. You get to stand right smack on the same hallowed turf as these legends of the links, and maybe even talk with them. Arnold Palmer once asked our advice about a shot at Augusta, took it, and missed the hole by miles.

You may not ever succeed in perfecting your own swing, but you have the inalienable right to criticize Lee Trevino's, which, as any book will tell you, is all wrong.

The big difference between the professional and the amateur is that the pros have probably played a course over and over, and prior to a tournament they go out and hit a few hundred practice drives, approach shots, and putts. They play like high-tech robots. When things go wrong, it's only because a spectator coughed, a camera flashed, a gnat's flight created turbulence, or the vindictive god of the greens hexed the ball into an improbable bounce. It happened to you last week in the same place, and you could have told them if only they'd asked.

There have been many great ones—Ben Hogan, "Babe" Zaharias, Bobby Jones, Kathy Whitworth, Arnold Palmer. To the casual observer, all they did was hit the ball with grace and purpose. To those who play golf, they were Merlins, the stuff of myth. The pros have a lock on the esoteric secret of golf—a secret of which we only occasionally have a tantalizing taste. Hitting the ball sweetly onto the green in two and then making the putt. It's a shame that the pros do this all the time. It must be tedious.

GOLF HUMOR

Funny game, golf,
especially the way I play it.

Henry Cooper

Because humor comes hard to the golfer (a miserable wretch at the best of times), golf stories tend to exhibit sick humor – pretty much on the same level as dead-baby jokes. There are very few of the classics that don't mention, or at least hint at, death or destruction. Since the same stories are told all over the world, you'd better know the standard ones so you can stop other golfers from telling them – which they will do at the slightest provocation. Most classic golf stories concern fanatical dedication to the game.

(1) Golf Pro: "Keep a firm grip on the club, fingers overlapping. Keep your head still and your eye on the ball. Now hit it smoothly . . ." The golfer hits the ball hard, but it slices to the right over the fence and into a road, where it hits a biker on the head. The biker swerves toward an oncoming car and ends up in the ditch. The car swerves to avoid the biker and heads toward a bus, which veers to the other side of the road and turns over. The golfer, in great distress, yells, "What should I do? What should I do?" Calmly

the golf pro answers, "Keep your right elbow closer to your side as you follow through."

(2) Three golfers go out for their weekly game. On the second green, one of them has a heart attack and drops dead. Later in the clubhouse the pro comes up to them to offer his condolences. "I'm really sorry. It must have ruined your day!" "No," one of them replies, "but it was a pain in the neck. For the last sixteen holes it was hit the ball, drag Fred, hit the ball, drag Fred . . ."

(3) A woman is about to putt out when a funeral procession passes by. She stops, bows her head, and stands silent. "Gee, Gladys," says one of her pals, "I didn't know you were so religious. Do you do that every time you see a funeral?" "Nope," Gladys replies, "but he *was* a good husband."

(4) A golfer with heat exhaustion is rushed to the hospital by ambulance. As they're wheeling him in on the gurney, the intern is taking his temperature. "It's 103. No, now it's 104." The golfer looks up, grasps the intern's jacket, and pleads, "Doc, Doc, ya gotta tell me. What's par for heatstroke?"

(5) A golfer falls into a lake and cries out to her fellow players, "Help, help, I'm drowning!" "Don't worry," one yells back, "you won't drown. You can't keep your head down long enough for that!"

(6) Father O'Flaherty drives into his fourth sand trap of the first nine. He takes a mighty swing and the ball dribbles down the slope of the trap and lands four feet away. Grimly he breaks his club

across his knee and buries the pieces in the sand trap. Then, without a word, he rips his golf bag to shreds and flings them and the remainder of his clubs and balls in the woods. "Patrick," he remarks to his companion with a deep sigh, "I'm going to have to give it up." "Golf?" Patrick asks. "No," O'Flaherty replies, "the priesthood."

It's up to you as a bluffing golfer to mine for some new material. A good joke, told at the right time (like just before your opponent begins the downswing on the first tee), might net you several strokes on the front nine. Most golf jokes are best reserved, however, as a means of alleviating the gloom of the clubhouse.

GOLF LITERATURE

Golf is a terrible game.
I'm glad I don't have to play again until tomorrow.

Anon.

There are basically two kinds of books on golf, instructional and inspirational. Give the former to anyone you're likely to play with. It's been astutely said that there's not much you can learn from books of instruction by the great professionals. They just don't know what it feels like to be you. Try to do all the things they recommend and you'll end up in the hospital or on a psychiatrist's couch. So shower your golfing friends with books like *Sixty Easy Ways to Improve Your Swing* and *Golfing Made Easy* because nothing will throw them farther off course (literally). Our friend Clyde has a roomful of books on how to play golf. He had to buy a ladder the other day so he could reach the top ones in his bookcase. He fell off the ladder and was unable to play for two weeks. He reads a new one each week and avidly waits for his monthly copy of *Golf Digest* to appear. Each week he gets a little more confused. For Christmas we're sending him *Zen Putting*.

The inspirational books, on the other hand, while they don't actually do anything for your game, don't do much to hurt it either. They simply keep you psychologically revved enough so you can keep on truckin' down the fairway toward your next fateful round. The number of inspirational golf books comes in second only to the number of self-help volumes. They all seem to have titles like *The Golfer's Bedside Book*, with disjointed essays written in an alcoholic haze by well-loved commentators and the ghosted autobiographies of the great. Although these lyrical nostalgia trips bring us back to the rolling fairways each week, there's a yawning abyss between reality and the rosy fog of memory. Most golf matches are really very prosaic occurrences, and you generally couldn't differentiate one from another, but memories of them, committed to paper, are effusively poetic and full of human conflict, drama, and angst. They're loaded with reminiscences of trivia, such as how Archie Compton beat Walter Hagen in 1928, which don't do our golf a speck of good but that offer us a fool's paradise of inspiration. If Hagen could find the silver lining in his thundercloud of defeat, we reason, then so can we.

Study golfing literature selectively to arm yourself with a dozen or so effective facts. For example, when your opponent explains the perfect putt he just made by saying it's just like Hogan's style, you can remind him that Varden did just the opposite. He'll never have absolute confidence in his stance again. Do this often enough and the erosion will become permanent and extensive. You may be on your way to producing the perfect golfing companion.

THE YELLOW BRICK ROAD

I'm hitting the driver so good
I gotta dial the operator for long distance after I hit it.

Lee Trevino

What golfer hasn't stepped out onto some glorious golf course on a sunny spring morning, the dew dewing on each blade of grass, the sparrows improvising overhead, the air like a whiff of newly baked bread. Suppose, to add fantasy to mere euphoria, that it's one of those heaven-planned courses like Augusta, where the back nine is a constant visual flirtation. Where many of the holes aren't crafty man-made contrivances but whole, unsullied grasslands gently fashioned out of the natural flow of the earth. But you might conjure equally as well a course carved out of the Rockies or the Hawaiian lava flows, running through the evergreen glades of Florida or up the pebbled coast of California, lying in postcard perfection in Portugal or Spain, or appearing startlingly in the Australian outback or the African veldt. On crisp clear mornings each of these courses, made for human delight, is simply good to be upon. They challenge you to a game. The rabbits jump, the crows screech, the hawks glide overhead.

The clubhouse flag flaps lazily. The irons in their ranks in the golf bag are polished and ready for the fight. The golfer's hands clasp naturally in an easy practice grip. The newly unwrapped ball is as white and shining as a Colgate ad. You can almost hear the distant roar of applause as the ball bounds onto the green and clips the pin. This is what it's all about.

Isn't it?

GLOSSARY

Address—A good address is considered essential to golf. Like "18 Fairway Drive," "Par Avenue," or "Link's View Lane." There's also the more technical meaning of moving body and club to the ball. Once you've wiggled your head once or twice, shuffled your feet, twitched your rear, shifted into a straight-backed, barstool posture, waggled the club, and brought its head to the ground, you've addressed the ball. Sort of said "yo" to it. If after all that, you fall over backwards or the ball does, you've made a shot.

As it lies—Playing the ball from the place where it has, by the laws of nature, come to rest. This is almost always in a gully or behind a luxuriant pine tree. You can overcome such a difficulty by a general agreement to play "winter rules," which means you can pick up the ball, clean it, and replace it on any convenient mound. Winter rules have been known to extend from August 1st through June 30th on the theory that it's winter *somewhere.*

Baffy—Ancient name for a 4-wood. Even experienced, professional caddies can be stumped by a request for a baffy.

Balls—Correct response to an opponent who suggests that you inadvertently touched the ball in addressing it and therefore should lose a stroke.

Birdie – A term denoting the score on a hole of one under par. Ornithological origins uncertain.

Blaster – Type of stroke used by Clyde when in any sort of hazard. Also the early term for a sand wedge.

Bogey – Taking more strokes on a hole than par; bogey, double bogey, triple bogey, etc. Called a bogey because all golfers are haunted by the thought of it.

Brassie – An archaic name for the 2-wood. Also the term for the voice of a woman you're inevitably paired with when you go out to the course as a single.

Caddie – To use a caddie is a great mark of distinction. Not because you can afford one but because you play well enough not to be distracted by his flippant advice and/or badly muffled guffaws.

Cleek – Either (a) a shallow-faced iron corresponding to the modern 2-iron or (b) the bunch that run the golf course and think they own it.

Dogleg – A hole (fairway) which bends right or left tempting the player to cut the corner (usually with disastrous results). A lot of golfers' troubles stem from their doglegs.

Draw – Either (a) a shot that deliberately moves out to the right and then in again towards the fairway or green (the opposite of fade) or (b) the amateur's description of what his opponent describes as a hook.

Driver, Drive – The driver is a wooden club with the most perpendicular face, also known as the 1-wood. Meant to send the ball the maximum distance, it's also the one most likely to send it in the wrong direction or into the ground, so most amateurs prefer to use a 2- or 3-wood. Many drive with an iron, so the two terms are not intimately connected.

Eagle – A score for a hole that's two less than par. It's called an eagle because it's a very rare bird.

Fade – Either (a) a shot that deliberately moves out to the left and then in again toward the fairway or green (the opposite of draw), (b) the amateur's description of what a more critical person would describe as a slice, or (c) what the elderly and overweight golfer starts to do around the 14th hole on a hot day.

Fairway – The parts of the course where anything that goes wrong is the golfer's own fault.

Fore! – A warning cry, yelled either just too late to prevent an insurance claim, or too early in the over-optimistic expectation that the ball will travel far enough to hit a distant group of players.

Gimmie – A putt of a length which the player thinks his opponent couldn't possibly miss and therefore doesn't have to attempt. There's no fixed length and a great deal of difference between what's expected (two or three feet) and what's conceded (two or three inches). After a gimmie, for some inexplicable reason, most players still try to putt out and often miss, though they claim to have won the hole, which greatly upsets their opponent.

Green – An area of smooth grass with a hole in the bumpy part.

Ground under repair – Condition of those parts of the course where some golfer had a hard time.

Hazard – Standing anywhere in front of a rank amateur as he takes a shot (richochets off tee markers, trees, and golf carts make the hazard a 360-degree problem). Any deliberately devised trap for the unwary.

Holed out – A term meaning that the ball has gone in.

Hook – A shot that veers right, then goes wildly out to the left. Players more commonly refer to it as a draw.

Iron – Originally this was a special name for a metal-headed club with a fairly straight face that might now be referred to as a 3-iron. Today the term *iron* categorizes all metal-headed clubs that aren't woods (many of which are now confusingly made of metal).

Jigger – Long-obsolete name for an iron with a narrow blade. Today's equivalent is the 4-iron. The name comes from the remark made by one golfer whenever he used it and observed the result. "Well I'll be jiggered." While your opponent is trying to figure out what a jigger is, his mind can appreciably wander from the game.

Lie – Either where the ball comes to rest or where the player claims it came to rest.

Lost ball – What a ball is said to be if it disappears in the bushes and isn't found within five minutes. Some of the uncivilized, ignorant players take ten minutes. A ball about to be played by Clyde could almost certainly be predesignated as a lost ball. Normally Clyde is asked, "Why do you keep using a new ball when you're only going to lose it? Why don't you use an old one?" To which Clyde says, "Because I've never *had* an old one". (Deep sigh.)

Mashie—An iron club. In its heyday, hickory shafted, it became the golfer's favorite iron. Some used it for practically everything, even when it became more commonly known as a 5-iron. There was also a *spade mashie,* nearer to a 6-iron, and a *mashie-niblick,* which was more like a 7.

Niblick—A golf club with a very sloping face (now commonly called a 9-iron), introduced by the English Lord Niblick in 1862. It was a mashie when he started the game, but he was a violent man. When asked at the end of a round, "What do you call that thing?" he replied, rather rudely, "Call it a #!!*#*! niblick if you want!"

Par—The score per hole that's considered reasonably within the reach of an ordinary adult. The amateur is pleased with par, but professionals are unhappy if they don't get a birdie. Golfers, unlike most, generally feel good if they're under par.

Playing through—It's considered polite, when looking for a lost ball or otherwise bringing play to a halt, to allow those behind on the fairway to play through. For some reason there's a 75 percent chance that those playing through will hit duff shots and end up in a similar position. This causes much confusion and animosity.

Putting—What ought to be the easiest part of golf, when the ball is lying on the smooth, level grass of the green and needs only a well-judged shot to go in the hole. Unfortunately it's where most hearts are broken—when, for example, you've arrived on the green in three and then take another three to get down. There are endless, anguished conversations about break and line and much self-analysis. Some players use the putter off the green, in which case it's not called a putter but a Texas wedge.

Ray, Ted – golfer (1877-1947). When asked for advice on how to hit the ball farther, he replied, "Hit the thing harder!"

Sand Trap – Also called a bunker. A hole full of sand and an occasional poisonous creature with no legs or many legs. It features a deep, overhanging face on the side nearest the green and is where 25 percent of golf shots end up. When playing a ball in a sand trap, you must not allow the head of the club to touch the sand prior to the shot. Your opponents and Big Brother will be watching.

Scratch player – A person not to be spoken to by the ordinary golfer until the scratch player's spoken first.

Shank – A disaster that happens to golfers who stand too close to their balls.

Slice – A shot that goes out to the left in a great arc and ends up on the right side of the fairway. Most slicers refer to their hits as fades.

Spoon – A wooden-headed club with a sloping face (equivalent to a modern 3-wood).

Stance – A peculiar and unnatural way of standing recommended by teaching pros.

Tee – Either the area defined by various white, yellow, or red plastic markers (at some clubs, big plastic golf balls), where you begin to attack each hole, or a small peg with a recessed top made of wood or plastic (often with "Get Back into Life" or some other poorly timed exhortation written on it) on which the ball is placed. This elevates it from the ground before you drive. (See *Driver*) From this you get "tee-hee," an expression used by those watching when you miss the ball.

Topping – Not the whipped cream, fudge, cherry, or nuts that you put on desserts. In golf, it means hitting the ball on its top rather than in its middle (where you should), so it runs along the ground before coming to rest behind a boulder.

Twitch – Putter's disease. Said to be incurable except by regular injections of alcohol.

Whiff – This has nothing to do with the cow pasture that's adjacent to the golf course. A whiff occurs when the golfer misses the ball completely, which is better than barely hitting it on the side, sending it in bizarre and unpredictable trajectories. The whiffing golfer's opponents will insist that he add a stroke to his score. The player will insist it's a practice swing, and a bitter argument will break out.

Woods – Wooden-headed clubs, increasingly made of metal. Like irons, they have numbers. 1-wood (driver), 2-wood (brassie), 3-wood (spoon), 4-wood (baffy), 5-wood (baffier). Nowadays the repertoire has been increased, ranging up to an 8-wood.

Words of W. C. Fields – The definitive comment on the game of golf. "Give me a beautiful day, a lovely golf course, and a gorgeous blonde, and you can keep your beautiful day and lovely golf course."

Bluffer's Guides
CENTENNIAL PRESS

The biggest bluff about the *Bluffer's Guides* is the title.
These books are full of information — and fun.

NOW IN STOCK — $3.95
Bluffer's Guide to Bluffing
Bluff Your Way in British Theatre
Bluff Your Way in Computers
Bluff Your Way in Hollywood
Bluff Your Way in Japan
Bluff Your Way in Management
Bluff Your Way in Music
Bluff Your Way in the Occult
Bluff Your Way in Paris
Bluff Your Way in Public Speaking

NEW TITLES
Bluff Your Way in Baseball
Bluff Your Way in the Deep South
Bluff Your Way in Football
Bluff Your Way in Golf
Bluff Your Way in Gourmet Cooking
Bluff Your Way in Marketing
Bluff Your Way in New York
Bluff Your Way in Wine

AVAILABLE SOON
Bluff Your Way in Basketball
Bluff Your Way in Office Politics
Bluff Your Way in Dining Out
Bluff Your Way in Fitness
Bluff Your Way in Home Maintenance
Bluff Your Way in Las Vegas
Bluff Your Way in London
Bluff Your Way in Marriage
Bluff Your Way in Parenting
Bluff Your Way in Psychology
Bluff Your Way in Sex

To order any of the Bluffer's Guides titles, use the order
form on the next page.

Get Bluffer's Guides at your bookstore or use this order form to send for the copies you want. Send it with your check or money order to:

Centennial Press
Box 82087
Lincoln, NE 68501

Title	Quantity	$3.95 Each
Total Enclosed		

Name_____

Address_____

City _____

State_____ Zip_____